Norse Mythology

Thor, Odin, Loki, and the Other Gods and Heroes

© **Copyright 2015 by From Hero To Zero Publishing - All rights reserved.**

This document is geared towards providing exact and reliable information in regards to the topic and issues covered. The publication is sold with the idea that the publisher is not required to render accounting, officially permitted, or otherwise, qualified services. If advice is necessary, legal or professional, a practiced individual in the profession should be ordered.

- From a Declaration of Principles which was accepted and approved equally by a Committee of the American Bar Association and a Committee of Publishers and Associations.

In no way is it legal to reproduce, duplicate, or transmit any part of this document in either electronic means or in printed format. Recording of this publication is strictly prohibited and any storage of this document is not allowed unless with written permission from the publisher. All rights reserved.

The information provided herein is stated to be truthful and consistent, in that any liability, in terms of inattention or otherwise, by any usage or abuse of any policies, processes, or directions contained within is the solitary and utter responsibility of the recipient reader. Under no circumstances will any legal responsibility or blame be held against the publisher for any reparation, damages, or monetary loss due to the information herein, either directly or indirectly.

Respective authors own all copyrights not held by the publisher.

The information herein is offered for informational purposes solely, and is universal as so. The presentation of the information is without contract or any type of guarantee assurance.

The trademarks that are used are without any consent, and the publication of the trademark is without permission or backing by the trademark owner. All trademarks and brands within this book are for clarifying purposes only and are the owned by the owners themselves, not affiliated with this document.

Table of Contents

Introduction 5

Chapter 1: Cosmology 6

Chapter 2: The Norse Pantheon 11

Chapter 3: The Creation 17

Chapter 4: The Fortification of Asgard 20

Chapter 5: Iduna's Apples 23

Chapter 6: Odin in Midgard 27

Chapter 7: Thor's Adventures Amongst the Giants 31

Chapter 8: The Curse of Gold 39

Chapter 9: The Death of Balder 52

Chapter 10: The End and the Beginning 56

Afterword: Sources 59

Introduction

Echoes of Norse mythology are everywhere in our art and popular culture. The Norse gods and heroes appear directly in stories from Wagner's epic opera cycle *Der Ring das Nibelung* to Neil Gaiman's dark novel <u>American Gods</u> to Douglas Adams' satirical novel <u>The Long Dark Tea-Time of the Soul</u> to the movie *Thor*. Fantasy writers including J.R.R. Tolkien, C.S. Lewis, Ursula Le Guin and Tad Williams have used story-patterns, obscure names and otherworldly creatures from the Norse myths in worlds of their own creation.

What were the original myths? Scholars are still debating that. The Old Norse poems and stories that survive are fragmented and sometimes contradictory. This book won't attempt to settle questions about authenticity, but only to offer a first look at some of the most enduring and influential characters and stories from Norse myths. Suggestions for further reading are in the "Sources" section at the end.

Chapter 1: Cosmology

The universe in which the Norse myths were set was strange, rich, dangerous, deceptive and impermanent. That universe began in chaos, was shaped in a series of cosmic battles, and took on a stable shape for a while. The gods who tried to rule it knew that they couldn't maintain order forever. During Ragnarok, the day of destruction, they would be overthrown by their enemies and the universe would be unmade. But they foresaw the beginning of a beautiful new world after their own deaths. Whether that new world would last forever was not altogether clear.

The creatures of this universe of myth were many and varied: not only men, animals and gods but also Norns, frost-giants, dwarves and elves. Many of these creatures were able to change their shape and appear in other forms. Any poor beggar or any animal may reveal itself as a powerful being in disguise. The gods and giants also had the gift of changing not only their own shapes but the appearance of the world, creating cities and landscapes of illusion. This gift didn't only allow them to dupe mortals; other giants and gods could themselves be deceived. For the gods were powerful but not omnipotent, strong but not safe from death, wise but not all-seeing. Mortals and immortals alike had to make their way through this unknown and unstable world as best they could.

The World Tree and Its Inhabitants

The universe was made up of nine worlds nestled among the roots and branches of the great World Tree, the ash tree Yggdrasil. Dragons and other beasts gnawed at the tree's roots. Odin and other immortals traveled from world to world along the tree's branches. Below the tree, almost completely inaccessible to the dwellers in the worlds, lay the Well of Destiny- also called the Well of Wisdom. Three Norns, beautiful and immortal women, watered the World Tree from that well; they also carved magical runes into its trunk which determined the fate of the Nine Worlds.

In some tales the Nine Worlds seem to be clearly separated from one another. In others they seem to overlap, so that beyond the protective enclosures of Asgard and Midgard the dangerous wastes of Jotunheim stretch.

Asgard was the bright and beautiful home-world and fortress of the Aesir, the immortal tribe which contained the best-known gods and goddesses of the Norse pantheon. Odin, Frigga, Thor, Loki, Balder and many more lived here. It was connected to Midgard, the human world, by the celestial bridge Bifrost, the rainbow. Asgard was surrounded by a great wall to keep out the enemies of the Aesir, especially the frost-giants of Jotunheim. Within Asgard many of the deities had their own palaces which reflected their own character.

Midgard was the human world, built by the Aesir Gods. Like Asgard, it was surrounded by a defensive wall. The rainbow bridge Bifrost connected Midgard and Asgard. Humans could only cross the bridge after they died, but the gods could and sometimes did cross into the human world at will. The enclosed land where Midgard's people lived was completely surrounded by an impassable, serpent-infested sea.

Most of the Norse legends were set in Asgard or Midgard, the only two worlds accessible to humans. Many of them featured beings from the other seven worlds that travelled more freely than humans could.

Jotunheim was the home of the Jotunns or frost-giants, enemies of the Aesir gods since the creation of the world. Like the gods, they had great physical strength and considerable magical power. Unlike the gods, they were mostly hostile to humans and to order and civilization; the Norse word usually translated as 'giant' means 'devourer'. However there were commerce deals and marriages as well as war between the giants and the gods, and the gods were partly descended from the giants (see the Creation story below). Jotunheim was a frozen wilderness, full of dark forests and steep mountains.

Vanaheim was the home of the Vanir, the non-Aesir tribe of gods. There was war between the tribes of gods when they first met, but instead of continuing to fight they exchanged hostages and made a treaty of peace.

Njord and his children Freyja and Freyr came to Asgard as hostages and are featured in some of the myths.

Svartalfheim was the home world of the beings called Dwarves or Dark Elves. These beings weren't necessarily small in size like the dwarves we imagine now. They were master craftsmen and makers of magical objects including Thor's hammer, Freyja's necklace, and Freyr's warship. The warship always found a favorable wind, it could carry immense numbers when need but it could also be folded up and tucked into a pocket. They Dwarves or Dark Elves lived underground.

Alfheim was the home world of the Elves, rather mysterious presences in the Norse myths. They were immortal, immensely beautiful and drawn to beauty.

Helheim or **Hel** was the underworld, the world of the dead who didn't end up in one of the palaces of the Aesir gods. Despite the name it wasn't much like the Hell of the Abrahamic religions; the name simply meant 'hidden'. There were descriptions of the way to Hel--through dark valleys, over a furious river and a narrow bridge, and then (for gods or heroes intending to visit Hel and come back alive) over the wall instead of through the gate; what lay inside the wall wasn't clearly described. One poem described murderers, oath breakers and adulterers as being imprisoned in a cold, dark hall of Hel which was infested by venomous snakes and wolves. Another mentions a great hall of feasting in Hel where Balder the Beloved was taken after his death.

Niflheim was the world of cold and ice, one of the two primal worlds that existed before the cosmos. Some legends suggest that it was the same as Hel, but others contradict that.

Muspelheim was the other primal world- the world of heat and fire, home of Surt and the fire-demons.

Chapter 2: The Norse Pantheon

The Gods:

Odin, also called Woden or Wotan, was the god of inspiration and the giver of poetry, wisdom and battle-rage. Most of the myths describe him as the firstborn and father of the gods, although some older stories give that role to Tyr. He was also the war-leader of the gods as they sought to defend themselves against the giants. He gathered the souls of human heroes killed in battle and brought them to his castle Valhalla. While the universe lasted, these warriors shared in endless feasting and also in friendly combat designed to keep them fit for the final battle against the giants and monsters at Ragnarok. In his other castle, Valaskjalf, stood a throne from which he could see everything that happened in the Nine Worlds.

Odin was a perpetual seeker after wisdom. He gave up his right eye as the price for a drink of the Water of Wisdom from the Well of Destiny. He wounded himself, hung upside down and fasted on Yggdrasil, the World Tree, for nine days and nights in order to prove himself worthy of learning the runes of the magical alphabet with which the Norns shaped the fate of the universe.

Odin was one of the three gods who created the world and gave life to humans. He often disguised himself and took long and dangerous journeys from his throne among the gods through the worlds of men and giants.

Thor, the son of Odin and the giantess/goddess Jord (whose name means 'earth'), was the strongest of the gods and a loyal and formidable defender of Asgard. He wielded the battle-hammer Mjollnir, the lightning, and in difficult situations he tended to strike out with it before stopping to think. His impulsivity landed him in many difficult situations, but his strength and courage usually got him safely out of them. Thor was called upon to bless weddings and also the planting of crops.

Loki was a clever and baffling god. He was very good at devising ways of getting what he wanted in the short term, but he apparently didn't consider long-term consequences. He sometimes helped the giants to deceive or rob the gods and then helped the gods to get their own back. (See "The Apples of Youth" below for one example of this pattern.) He was a shape-changer, appearing sometimes as a hawk, a fly, a human, a giantess or a mare. Some versions of the creation myth say he was one of the three gods who created humans.

Over time Loki's role became more clearly hostile to gods and humans. He schemed to get Balder killed. At Ragnarok he led the attack against the gods, followed by the great wolf Fenris and the Midgard Serpent, who were his children from a love-affair with a giantess.

Balder, son of Odin and the goddess Frigga, was the wisest, gentlest, most eloquent and most beautiful of the gods. He lived in Breidablikk, the Peace Stead, where nothing evil could enter. He heard disputes and gave fair judgments which could not be changed; after he died his son Forsete took over this role.

Njord was the ruler of the wind, the tamer of fire, floods and storms and the giver of wealth. He was one of the hostages given to the Aesir as a pledge of peace, along with his children Freyr and Freyja. Later his marriage to the giantess Skadi avoided a blood-feud (see 'Iduna's Apples" below).

Tyr was a god of strength, sound judgment, courage and oath-keeping, often called on by warriors and seekers of wisdom. He is honorably mentioned in the later Norse myths; he may have been the ruler of the gods in the earlier legends.

When the gods persuaded Loki's son, the incredibly strong and vicious wolf Fenris, to let them test his strength by binding him with a cord, Fenris agreed only on the condition that he should be released again if he couldn't free himself. As a guarantee of this Fenris asked one of the gods to leave his hand in his mouth until Fenris was freed. Tyr was the only god willing to do this. Fenris, of course, was not freed, and Tyr, of course, lost his hand.

Honir was the brother and companion of Odin and, in some of the stories he was one of the creators of mankind. He was one of the few gods destined to survive Ragnarok.

Frey or Freyr, son of Njord and brother of Freyja, was another of the Vanir who stayed with the Aesir as a hostage and peace-pledge. He was the god of sun, rain and harvest.

Heimdall was the guardian of the rainbow bridge, the entrance to Asgard.

Bragi was the god of eloquence and flowing speech, prayed to by all skalds (bards). He welcomed heroes to Valhalla with stirring songs and tales of battle. His wife was Iduna, keeper of the Apples of Youth.

Goddesses:

The Norns were not exactly goddesses and did not live in Asgard, but they were perhaps the most powerful beings in the Norse cosmos. They were described as white-skinned and extremely beautiful women. Some of them were descended from gods, others from elves or dwarves. Three of them kept the World Tree alive and carved the runes that determined the fate of the universe, as described above. Lesser

Norns wove the fates of individual mortals. Like the gods and goddesses, the Norns could be kind or cruel; which sort of Norn was assigned to any particular mortal seemed to be a matter of chance. There are no detailed stories about individual Norns; their fate-weaving was shrouded in mystery.

The following were goddesses who ruled in Asgard:

Frigga was the wife of Odin and the mother of Balder. She knew the fates of all living things, though she seldom spoke of what she foresaw. Sometimes in the trance of prophecy she could alter the fates she read, although her power to do this was less than that of the Norn-women. She owned a magic hawk-feather cloak that allowed her and the other Aesir to shift into hawk-shape. She also sometimes appeared as a poor human woman in Midgard.

Freyja, daughter of Njord, was another of the Vanir hostages given to the Aesir to secure peace between them. She was the goddess of beauty and of love, and lovers prayed to her although her own love life was not altogether happy. She loved her husband Odr, who left her often for long journeys. She sought him for a long time in Midgard, and she wept red-gold tears for him. According to some stories, she was also glad to make love with any god or other being who was either attractive or willing to give her something she wanted. Like Frigga, Freyja had the gift of prophecy and also owned a cloak of falcon-feathers which let the wearer take the shape of a falcon. Some of the warriors who fell in battle went to Valhalla, and others joined the endless feast in Freyja's castle, Folkvang.

Iduna was the keeper of the Apples of Youth which gave the gods their immortality. Whenever the gods grew old they ate from Iduna's magic apples and became young again.

Hel was the ruler of Helheim, the world of the dead.

Var was the goddess who heard and remembered all the oaths that mortals swore to each other, and punished those who broke their oaths.

Not quite goddesses, but still powerful, were the **Valkyries**. These were Odin's helpers for the most part, although they were clearly capable of defying him- there's more about that in the tale of the Cursed Hoard below. The Valkyries were immortal, beautiful, strong, magically skilled and ferocious shield-maidens who attended the combats of mortals. Their magic determined which warriors lived and which were killed. They also took the souls of particularly brave men killed in battle to Valhalla to join the feast at Odin's table.

Chapter 3: The Creation

Before there was sand, sea, sky, land or any living thing, there was Ginungagap. This was a vast abyss stretching between Muspelheim, the place of pure fire and melting heat, and Niflheim, the place of deep cold and grinding ice.

The fire-world and the ice-world grew in power. From Muspelheim flames licked out farther and farther into the emptiness, and from Niflheim ice-rivers crept into the void, slowly but irreversibly. When flame and ice met water flowed free and great steams arose, but as the cold struck them they fell back into ice again. From these changing waters Ymir, the first and greatest of the frost-giants, took shape and from his sweat newer and smaller frost-giants arose.

Still the heat grew stronger, and the cow Audhumbla was formed from the melting ice. Ymir and his children drank her milk, and she herself was nourished by licking the salty ice. As she licked she freed another being trapped in the ice, a very handsome figure called Buri - the first of the gods, whose son was Borr. Borr married Bestla, one of Ymir's daughters, and their children were Odin and his brothers. Buri and Bor vanish from the stories after Odin's birth.

Odin and his brothers killed Ymir and from his body they built the worlds; his flesh became earth, his bones rock, and his blood the water of the rivers and oceans. Most of the giants died in the floods that rose as Ymir's blood spilled, but a few escaped to the cold wilderness of Jotunheim.

The gods built Midgard, the human world, inside a protective wall made from Ymir's eyebrows. They took sparks from Muspelheim and threw them into the sky to shine as stars. From that fire they also made the sun and moon, and they appointed Sol and her brother Mani to drive the chariots which carried the sun and moon across the sky marking days, months and years. Behind the chariots ran two ravenous wolves, eager to devour the light and its protectors. The gods did not destroy those wolves, but the chariots were so swift that the wolves could not overtake them until the end of the worlds and the gods at Ragnarok.

Now there was order where there had been chaos, and the worlds grew with green plants and other living beings. Maggots had begun to breed in Ymir's body before the work of creation was finished, and these were given the gift of life and will and became the race of dwarves. In Midgard three of the gods took two trees and formed them into the first human beings. Ask, the first man, came from the ash tree and Embla, the first woman, from the elm. Odin gave them living souls. According to some stories, Honir gave them their five senses and Loki gave them warmth and color. Other stories leave Loki out and say that Odin was helped by his brothers Vili and Ve, who don't come up much in the rest of the mythology.

Chapter 4: The Fortification of Asgard

The gods established life, order and beauty in their own world of Asgard. They made high buildings and strong citadels, including Valhalla of the warriors and Valaskjalf from which Odin watched over all that happened in the nine worlds. They met and made peace with the gods of Vanaheim after initial suspicion. According to some of the stories Honir, one of the creators of humankind, went to Vanaheim as a peace-pledge while Njord, Freyja and Freyr of the Vanir came to stay in Asgard. There was much joy in Asgard, but there was fear as well. The gods could not forget that Ymir's children held a grudge against them and might attack at any time. So they were overjoyed when a builder came to them, offering to raise them a great wall as a sure defense against the giants.

The builder's promise was tempting; all the more so as he promised to complete the work within two winters and a summer but the price he asked was terribly high. He asked for Freyja's hand in marriage, and also for the sun and moon. Freyja was quite unwilling to marry him, and the gods feared to lose both her beauty and the light and order they had made. But someone-and when the gods tried to remember the matter later they agreed it must have been Loki-suggested that they accept the builder's offer, with conditions. All the work had to be done by the builder himself and all had to be completed within one winter; if anything was left unfinished on the first day of summer, the builder would go unpaid. The gods believed that the builder could never complete his task in time, so they made the offer. The builder accepted, with one condition of his own: that his stallion could help him haul stone. The gods agreed, and many oaths were sworn.

But what a stallion that was! He was strong and tireless and got more work done than his master, and three days before the beginning of summer all the wall was built except for the gate. There seemed to be no doubt about the builder finishing his work on time.

Then the gods, especially Freyja, regretted their bargain. They feared that the builder had come from Jotunheim, meaning to take away the light and the loveliness of their home without having to fight for it. They decided that Loki had made the suggestion which was about to ruin them, and they threatened Loki with torment and death if he didn't find some way to stop the work from being finished on time. Loki begged the gods for mercy and promised to do whatever it took to prevent the work being from completed and the builder's price paid. Then he left the citadel alone.

That night when the builder took his stallion with him to haul stone, they heard the whinnying of a mare in the darkness ahead and the stallion caught the mare's scent. He neighed with joy, broke his reins and galloped off into the night, following the mare who ran away from him, deeper and deeper into the woods. The builder chased the horses, shouting and cursing, but they left him far behind.

That morning there was no stone ready for the builder to raise around the gates, and he builder knew that he had lost his wager. In his anger he took his true form, and the gods saw that he was indeed a giant of Jotunheim just as they had feared. Thor was furious and struck the giant with his hammer, killing him at once.

A few months later Loki, in the shape of the fleet-footed and beautiful mare who had led the stallion astray, gave birth to a grey foal with eight legs who was the best horse in the worlds. Odin took that horse for his own, and he rode it ever after along the roots and branches of the great World Tree.

Chapter 5: Iduna's Apples

On one occasion Odin, Honir and Loki, the three who had made humankind, traveled over mountains and fields into a country they did not know. After long journeying they were hungry, and when they found a herd of oxen grazing they slaughtered one and set about cooking it but the meat remained raw. They argued about why this had happened until the eagle who had sat hidden in the branches above them called to them and said that his magic kept the meat from cooking. If they gave him a portion of the meat, he said, their food would cook and they could eat.

The gods, tired and hungry, agreed but the eagle swooped down and took the best parts of the meat. Loki, who was never noted for his patience, tore a great branch from the tree and swung it at the eagle. The eagle seized the other end of the pole and lifted the branch, Loki and all, into the sky and flew far from Loki's companions. Loki cried out in terror, and the eagle said that he would never set Loki down again until Loki promised to bring him both Iduna and her Apples of Youth from Asgard.

Now this was a dangerous promise for it was only Iduna and her apples that kept the gods from death; whenever they felt old age stealing over them they ate of her apples and grew young again. But Loki was afraid for his life, so he made his promise and rejoined his companions.

On returning to Asgard, Loki went to Iduna and told her that on his travels he had found a marvelous apple tree whose fruits she would greatly admire. Perhaps, he said, they were better than the apples she had. He suggested that she bring her apples to the new tree so they could make a comparison. Iduna was a trusting goddess, and she agreed and went with Loki. They traveled together out of sight of Asgard's walls and into the wild country, where the eagle swooped down from the sky and carried both Iduna and her apples away to his home in the wild mountains of Jotunheim. There he took on his true shape again, revealing himself as the wealthy and powerful giant Thiassi.

In Asgard the gods felt old age stealing over them, leaving gray in their hair and weariness in their bones and they had no remedy. Many of the gods assembled and asked each other what could have become of Iduna and where she had last been seen. The last that any god had seen or heard was that she had gone away with Loki.

Loki was brought by force into the assembly and once again threatened with pain and death if he did not bring Iduna back. Fearing for his life, he made his promise to them as he had to Thiassi and asked for the loan of Freyja's falcon-feather cloak so that he might change his shape and fly. Freyja gave him what he asked for, and he flew swiftly and lightly to Jotunheim where he waited until Thiassi was gone far out to sea. Then he changed Iduna and her apples together into the shape of a nut, and picked them up and flew on the wings of the wind back toward Asgard. But Thiassi took on his eagle shape and flew after them, gaining at every beat of his wings which were longer and stronger than Loki's.

The gods looked out from the walls of Asgard and saw the falcon and the eagle coming. They piled tinder atop the walls. As soon as the falcon crossed the wall in a last desperate burst of speed, the gods fired the tinder so that flames caught in the pursuing eagle's wings. Thiassi fell to the ground in eagle shape and was killed.

Thiassi had a daughter named Skadi, a giantess both strong and brave. When she heard of her father's death she was furious, and she armed herself and marched alone into Asgard vowing to avenge her father. But the gods, instead of attacking her, offered her ransom. She agreed to peace on three conditions. First, that the gods would set Thiassi's eyes into the sky as stars so that he would always be remembered. Second, that they would make her laugh, which she hardly thought possible. Third, that she might choose for herself a husband from among the gods.

The gods agreed to all. The first condition was easily met. The second was harder, but at last Loki succeeded by tying himself to one end of a rope and a billy-goat to another and engaging in a furious tug-of-war. When he fell into Skadi's lap she laughed despite herself. For her third request, the gods set the condition that they would come before her masked and cloaked with only their feet showing, and she should choose her husband thus. She saw a particularly beautiful pair of feet and thought they must belong to Balder, fairest of the gods, but when he uncloaked himself she saw instead Njord the sea-god, the calmer of winds and storms. For a time it seemed they might be content together. But when Njord came with her to her mountain home he hated the crying of the wolves and longed for the sea, and when she came to Njord's home on the seashore she hated the screaming of the seagulls and longed for the mountains, so she left him- not happy, perhaps, but at peace.

Chapter 6: Odin in Midgard

King Hrauthung, a ruler of the Goths in Midgard, had two young sons. One day when Agnar, the eldest and heir to the crown, was ten years old and his brother Geirroth was eight, they went out fishing together in a small boat. A wild wind rose and drove the boat far from shore. Far into the night they were blown across the sea, and in the darkness they were shipwrecked on an unknown coast. They might have died that night in the cold, but an old man and an old woman- two poor peasants, as it seemed- took them in, fed then and sheltered them. The weather grew steadily worse and the boat was beyond repair, so they princes stayed all winter with the old couple. The woman tended Agnar, while the man tended Geirroth and taught him wisdom. When spring came the peasants gave the princes a new boat and bade them farewell. Just before they set out to sea the old man whispered something in Geirroth's ear. The princes sailed away together, not knowing that their hosts had been Odin and Frigga in disguise.

The little boat made the return journey safely, and Geirroth was the first to jump out of the boat at their father's deserted landing-place. But instead of holding the boat steady so Agnar could climb out as well, he pushed the boat back out to sea as hard as he could saying, "Go thou now where evil may have thee!" The wind arose, and Agnar alone could not steer the boat which drifted far out to sea again. No one was there to see what Geirroth had done. When he came to his father's city he found that his father was dead- men hailed his return as a miracle and he was crowned the King. He grew up, married and had a son, whom he named Agnar after the brother he had betrayed.

One day, when little Agnar was ten years old, Odin looked out from Asgard toward Midgard and laughed. He told Frigga that her fosterling, the older Agnar, was living in a cave and begetting children with a giantess while his own fosterling, Geirroth, was a ruling king. "Yes, and what a king!" Frigga said angrily. "He tortures his guests if there are too many of them making demands on his hospitality."

Odin swore that this was a lie, but it was hard to be sure of such a thing-for while Odin on his high seat could see into all lands, he could not see everything at once. So Odin and Frigga made a wager, and Odin disguised himself as a traveling man and made ready to go back to Midgard. But Frigga, unbeknownst to him, sent her maidservant ahead to Geirroth warning that a dangerous enchanter was traveling the countryside; he could be recognized, she said, by the fact that no dog would leap at him.

Now Geirroth was not generally an inhospitable man, but when an old man in a dark-blue mantle came to the door and the dogs let him pass as though he were an accustomed guest the king was suspicious. He had his guards seize the stranger and hold him for questioning. The stranger gave his name as Grimnir, 'the hooded one,' but he refused to say more about himself no matter how the guards threatened him. So Geirroth had his guest bound hand and foot and set close between two blazing fires until he was willing to answer the king's questions.

For eight days and eight nights Grimnir was bound there, given nothing to eat or drink. The fires were gradually built up until the mantle burned on Grimnir's back, but still he said nothing. At last Agnar, the king's young son, saw what was being done and pitied the stranger. He brought Grimnir a full horn of mead, and he said that the king did wrong to hurt Grimnir when Grimnir had done him no harm.

Grimnir drank, and Grimnir spoke. He complained of his pain and of the men who had stood by and let him suffer. He praised Agnar for giving him a drink, and foretold that Agnar alone would rule the Goths. Then he began to speak of the beauty and strength of Asgard and its inhabitants. All this time Geirroth listened and said nothing. Grimnir cried out that the mighty gods themselves saw how Geirroth abused his guest, and that while the gods had once helped Geirroth, he was now under their curse and would soon die by the sword. Geirroth listened grimly with his sword half-drawn. At last Grimnir called on his godly power and named himself as Odin. At this Geirroth leapt up, sword in hand and hurried toward his prisoner, meaning perhaps to free him or perhaps to attack him. He had the chance to do neither. The sword fell from his hand, hilt down, and he fell on the sword and died. Odin disappeared. Agnar ruled the Goths for many years, and we may guess that he was kind to mysterious strangers.

Chapter 7: Thor's Adventures Amongst the Giants

I: Thor in Utgard

One day Thor and Loki, together with Thor's human servant Thialfi, traveled from Asgard toward the giant's city of Utgard. They traveled a long time in wild lands until they found a great hall standing in the midst of the wild forest. When they knocked at the door no one answered, but the door opened at Thor's touch and they spent the night in that hall, with Thor guarding the threshold. In the middle of the night they heard a terrible noise and felt the ground shaking under them, but the hall stood firm. When they went outside in the morning they saw what had caused the roaring sound. A huge giant lay snoring on the ground not far from the doors of the hall.

Thor took up his hammer, put on the magic belt that doubled his strength and prepared to defend himself and his companions. But the giant, when he woke, seemed friendly enough. He introduced himself as Skrymir, announced that he knew Thor already and invited the gods and their servant to accompany him. They agreed, though they were daunted when Skrymir asked where his glove was and they realized that his glove was the hall in which they had spent the night.

Skrymir offered to carry their provision sack as well as his own. All day they journeyed together, Thialfi and the gods struggling to keep up with Skrymir's great strides. Later that night, Skrymir lay down to sleep after telling the gods to untie the sack and take out their own provisions from it. But even Thor could not begin to loosen the knots of the sack. Hungry, angry and afraid, Thor struck at Skrymir's head as Skrymir lay sleeping. He struck hard but the hammer bounced off, and Skrymir blinked, half-woke, and said he thought a leaf had fallen on his head. Twice more Skrymir seemed to sleep and Thor struck at him to no avail. In the morning they were ready to part company with Skrymir, who gave them directions to the city of Utgard. He warned them, however, that the folk of Utgard were even larger than himself, and that Thor and his companions had better behave themselves and make no boasts while they were in that city.

The walls of Utgard were higher than cliffs, and the gate-bars were so strong that Thor could not lift them so they had to creep in between. When they came to the king's great hall which was indeed filled with giants of Skrymir's size, the giant king looked scornfully at them saying he supposed that the little man must be Thor, who had such a misleading reputation for strength. He added that if Thor and his friends wished to stay as guests in Utgard they had better be able to do something impressive to prove themselves worthy guests.

Loki claimed that he could eat faster than anyone else. A man named Loge was chosen as his opponent, and a great dish of meat was placed between them. Each man started eating from one end and they met in the middle, but Loki had eaten only the meat from his portion of the dish while Loge had eaten up the bones and the dish as well.

Thialfi offered to race with anyone that the king might choose. The racecourse was set and Thialfi ran fast enough, but his opponent, Huge, was twice as fast as he was.

The king declared himself unimpressed by Thor's companions and challenged Thor himself to redeem the gods' reputation for power. Thor offered to show both his strength and his drinking ability.

No opponent was chosen for Thor in the drinking contest, but he was given a drinking-horn-large, indeed, but not impossibly so-and urged to drink it down in three draughts or fewer. Thor drank mightily, but the liquid in the horn hardly seemed to go down at all.

The king, laughing, said that since Thor was such a small man he would ask him for no greater feat of strength than to pick up the king's cat. The cat was rather large, but Thor thought it quite manageable until he went to lift it. The cat was terribly heavy, and when with great strain he lifted its belly as high as his head the cat's feet were still on the floor. The king laughed again and mocked Thor's smallness and weakness and Thor, infuriated, said that little or not he would wrestle with any man there.

The king, however, said that Thor was not worthy or capable of wrestling with his fighting men and called out an old woman to wrestle him. Thor meant to be gentle with her at first but soon he saw that there was no need for that, for she was stronger than he and soon forced him to his knees. Greatly ashamed, Thor rose and re-joined his companions who were much laughed at but also well fed.

In the morning the gods and Thialfi took their leave. The king of the giants went out of the city with them, asking how they had liked their visit. Thor said that he had been clearly bested and was deeply shamed.

The king told him then that there was not a need for shame, for Thor and his companions had not been honestly beaten but deceived. When the giants heard of Thor's coming they were afraid, and they wove spells of illusion around themselves and their city so that they appeared much larger than they truly were. Skrymir was the king himself in disguise, and when Thor thought he struck at Skrymir's head he was truly striking at the mountain that Skrymir had set between Thor and himself. Everything within the city they had taken for Utgard was similarly disguised. Loki's opponent in the eating contest was no man or giant but wildfire itself. Thialfi's opponent in the race was the king's thought given bodily form. The great horn Thor failed to empty was the sea itself, and his great draughts from it terrified the giants and caused the ebbing and flowing of the tides. The cat was indeed no cat but the vast Midgard Serpent whose coils filled the sea that surrounds the world of men. And the old woman who outwrestled Thor was Old Age herself, who was stronger than any giant, god or man. The king said that Thor showed himself stronger in the tests than the giants had expected, and if ever Thor came to visit them again they would once again fall back on spells of illusion.

Thor raised his hammer against the king and against the city, but in a twinkling they were gone.

II: Thor the Bride

One day Thor awoke to find his lightning hammer Mjollnir missing. He was furious and the gods were afraid, for they had lost their best weapon and they feared who might seek to turn it against them. Thor went to Loki for help, and Loki went to Freyja to beg the loan of her falcon feather cloak. She told him he'd be welcome to it if it was made of silver or gold, and she hurried him off on his search.

Loki put on the cloak and flew in falcon shape to Jotunheim, the land of the giants, where he stopped at the great hall of Thrym who was one of their strongest and wealthiest leaders. There he took off the cloak and appeared in his true form to Thrym, who asked him how the gods fared and what Loki's business might be.

Loki, for once, gave him a straight answer saying that the gods did very ill and they missed Thor's hammer, and asked if Thrym had taken it. Thrym answered roundly that he had taken it and buried it deep in the earth, and that the gods would not see it again until they sent him Freyja to be his wife.

Loki flew back to Asgard, where Thor demanded news before Loki had time even to land and change his shape. Loki passed on the giant's demand. Thor hurried to Freyja and told her to hurry and get ready for her wedding, for they had no time to lose. Freyja snorted fiercely enough to shake the whole hall and burst her most beautiful and treasured necklace. She made it extremely clear that she was completely unwilling to marry the giant, and that she'd be shamed before all the gods if she even thought of such a thing. Thor, who wanted his hammer as badly as Freyja wanted to avoid the marriage, appealed to the other gods who met for an urgent council.

Heimdall, the guardian of the rainbow bridge, suggested that Thor and Freyja both could be satisfied and Asgard kept safe, if Thor dressed himself in bridal garments and went to the giants in Freyja's place. He carefully spelled out what Thor would need for his disguise including a bridal veil, Freyja's necklace and a pretty cap in place of his war-helm.

Thor was almost as outraged as Freyja had been, and he pleaded that all the gods would call him unmanly if he let himself be dressed in women's clothing. But Loki, who had a practical mind and no great use for honor, observed that if they didn't get Mjollnir back the giants would wield it against Asgard and the gods would be overthrown. So Thor let himself be persuaded, and Loki agreed to don women's clothes as well and travel to Thrym's hall as Thor's maidservant. They disguised themselves, set off in Thor's goat-drawn chariot and soon came to Thrym's hall.

Thrym was delighted at their coming, and told all the company that with all his wealth, a lovely bride like Freyja was the one thing he had lacked. As soon as the guests entered a great feast was served. Thrym was astonished to see his bride-to-be devour eight salmon and a whole ox and drink three barrels of mead; this, he said, was by far the hungriest maiden he'd ever heard of. Loki answered quickly that Freyja had not eaten for eight days because she longed so hotly for Jotunheim. Thrym, much encouraged, leaned closer to his bride intending to kiss her. Instead he leaped back the full length of the hall and asked why the maiden's eyes burned so even through her veil. Loki explained that Freyja had not slept for eight days because she longed so hotly for Jotunheim.

Thrym's sister chose that moment to step forward and ask for the rings from Freyja's fingers, which were apparently the customary gift a bride should make to her sister-in-law. Thrym cut across her, calling for Thor's hammer to be brought out so that he and Freyja could swear their wedding vows on it. He set the hammer on the bride's knees, among the folds of her beautiful gown.

Thor laughed, took up the hammer, and slew all the giants in that hall. Then he and Loki rode back to Asgard together, laughing.

Chapter 8: The Curse of Gold

On another occasion Odin, Honir and Loki went exploring together, but this time instead of the world of giants they wandered into the world of men. They came to a stream that had been dammed into a pool, and on the dam sat an otter with a freshly caught salmon. Loki threw a stone at the otter and killed it, and he laughed and congratulated himself on having secured both salmon and otter with one throw. When they came to a house they laid aside all their weapons and tokens of power, asked for lodging for the night and said that they brought their own food, showing Loki's kills.

But the master of the house, Hreidmar, was a powerful enchanter and when he saw the dead otter his face hardened. He called his sons Fafnir and Regin to him and said to them that their brother the otter was dead, and that these three travelers had killed him. They fell on the gods and bound them, and Hreidmar told them that they deserved to die for they had killed his son while he was in an enchanted disguise.

Now the gods had meant no such harm but the deed was done, and they promised that if Hreidmar freed them they would bring him whatever ransom he asked for. Hreidmar agreed to this, and oaths were sworn on both sides. Then he showed them the skin of the otter and told them both to fill and cover it with gold, and he would consider the blood-price paid.

Odin and Honir remained prisoners in Hreidmar's house, but Loki was sent out to bring back the ransom. He traveled to Svartalfheim, the home of the Dwarves or Dark-Elves, who were known for the treasures they wrought and collected. There he found a solitary fish playing in a stream. Now Loki looked closely at this fish as he had failed to look at the otter, and he thought it was more than it seemed. He snatched the fish up in his hands and told it that he would kill it unless it ransomed its life with all the gold it possessed.

Then the fish took on its true shape, that of the wealthy Dwarf Andvare, who took Loki home to the rock where he kept his treasure and gave him his entire hoard. Loki saw that Andvare kept his hand clenched around something, and he demanded to know what it was. Andvare opened his hand to show a small ring. He begged to be allowed to keep that, saying that if he only had that he would soon become a wealthy man again. Loki demanded the ring as well as the rest and Andvare handed it over in fear of his life, but he cursed the ring and said that ever afterward it would bring only evil to its possessor. At this Loki laughed and said that he was satisfied, as he did not mean to keep the ring himself.

Loki returned to Hreidmar's house and showed the treasure to Odin and Honir. Odin saw that

Andvare's ring was very beautiful, and he said that he would keep that for himself giving the rest of the gold as ransom. Loki gave it willingly and said nothing about the curse. Then Hreidmar was called in to count up his blood-money.

The gold Loki brought filled the otter-skin and almost covered it, but there was still a lip-hair left uncovered and Hreidmar said he did not count the ransom paid. Then Odin gave him Andvare's ring, and Hreidmar pronounced himself satisfied and freed his captives. Once Odin had taken up his spear again and Loki his enchanted shoes, they had nothing to fear from Hreidmar's enchantment so Loki told Hreidmar of Andvare's curse before they departed.

The curse acted quickly in the world of men. Hreidmar and his sons stood together after the gods were gone, and they looked at the ransom the gods had paid. They thought perhaps more of the gold than of their dead kinsman. Fafnir and Regin demanded their share of the blood-price, for Hreidmar had lost a son but they had lost a brother. Hreidmar, however, claimed all the treasure as his own. The brothers were angry and killed him. Regin then proposed to divide the treasure with his brother, but Fafnir said that he had killed his father already for the sake of the gold and he would not hesitate to kill his brother as well. Then Fafnir buried the treasure on the wild heath of Gnitta, took on the shape of a dragon and brooded over the hoard, while Regin fled to King Alf's court and plotted vengeance.

III. Revenges

Once Sigurd's sword Gram was forged, Regin urged Sigurd against the dragon again. Sigurd replied that before avenging Regin's wrongs or seeking wealth, he had his father's death to avenge. He went to King Alf and raised an army, and they set out in long ships to attack King Lyngi's land. A storm rose on the sea, and the ships were near sinking when Sigurd in the foremost ship saw an old man on a rocky island. The old man demanded to be taken on board, and Sigurd welcomed him. Then the waves calmed and a fair wind arose, and the ships glided swiftly over the sea as the old man passed on battle-lore to the young prince. When the ships made landfall the old man once again vanished without telling Sigurd that Odin had stood at his side.

The battle against Lyngi's folk was furious, but Sigurd's men had the victory thanks largely to Sigurd himself, who led the charge and killed Lyngi and his sons. The fleet went home heavy with the gold they had won.

King Alf and his people welcomed Sigurd home, but Regin met him with a cold and challenging look and asked if he now dared to honor his word and ride against the dragon. Sigurd, as cold and as proud, agreed.

Now other heroes had gone to attack the dragon, both on their own and in armies, and all of them were dead. Terror billowed around Fafnir like a foul scent in the air, and his great mouth spat deadly venom which neither shield nor armor could keep off. To wound Fafnir was a danger in itself, for the dragon's boiling blood burned.

Nevertheless Sigurd followed Regin into the wilderness to find the dragon. But when they saw the track where the great beast had dragged its belly along the way from its lair to the lake where it drank, Sigurd turned to Regin and said, "I thought you told me Fafnir was no larger than common for a dragon, but this track is marvellously great."

Regin replied that it hardly mattered, as of course Sigurd wouldn't be attacking Fafnir frontally. The dragon was a creature of habit and it used the same track always; so if Sigurd dug a pit in the path and hid in it he could easily stab it from underneath.

"What about that boiling blood?" Sigurd asked. Regin called him a coward, and an unworthy son of his father. Sigurd said no more but set to digging a pit while Regin hid himself.

As Sigurd dug an old man came by and asked what he was doing. Sigurd explained, and the old man told him to dig many pits to hold the dragon's blood lest he should drown in it. Sigurd did so, and Odin vanished.

As Sigurd finished digging he felt the earth shaking with Fafnir's approach, and he smelled the acid stink of dragon poison. But he stayed in his place, and when the dragon's belly scraped above him he drove his sword into it up to the hilts before springing free, bloody to the shoulder and in pain.

Fafnir's first agony shook the earth and shattered trees and stones, but then he lay more quietly and asked Sigurd his name and who had urged him on. When Sigurd answered truthfully Fafnir mocked him as a king's son with no kingdom. But he gave Sigurd good advice as well, if only Sigurd had heeded him. He warned that a heavy curse lay on the dragon hoard, and that Regin hated Sigurd even as he hated Fafnir. He urged Sigurd to ride swiftly away and be free of curse and hate alike. But Sigurd said that he feared no curse for all men had to die someday, and that he would not turn away from honor or from treasure. So Fafnir died and the curse passed on from him.

When the last quaking of Fafnir's death-tremors passed away Regin came out of his hiding place. He stared at the ground and muttered that Sigurd had killed his own brother, and that he himself was not blameless in the matter. Sigurd said that he himself had borne all the danger of the dragon slaying while Regin hid, but Regin claimed credit for the advice and the sword that he had given to Sigurd. He cut the dragon's heart out and told Sigurd to roast it and leave it for Regin as the blood-price for his brother's death. Then Regin lay down to sleep.

When Sigurd thought the heart might be done he put out his finger to touch it and the hot fat burned him; he sucked his finger to ease the pain, and as that morsel of the dragon's heart passed his lips he understood the speech of the birds in the broken tree behind him. They warned, as Fafnir had, that Regin had plotted both Fafnir's death and Sigurd's; they said that great wisdom would come to the eater of the dragon's heart, and they urged Sigurd to kill Regin, save his own life and keep both gold and wisdom for himself. Sigurd believed them and killed Regin in his sleep. The birds told him then that the dragon's gold would win him a worthy wife in the court of King Giuki, and they sang of a wise Valkyrie who lay on the high fells locked in an enchanted sleep.

Sigurd desired everything the birds described. He ate of the dragon's heart. He rode to the dragon's lair, took the accursed gold of the hoard and piled it on his horse. Then he rode away with a high heart to seek his fortune.

IV. Love and Deceit

Sigurd rode over the high fells until he saw a castle that burned bright as flame. Going in, he found an armored figure lying fast asleep. Sigurd cut the armor away with the sword Regin had forged for him. As the armor fell away he saw that the sleeper was a woman, and very beautiful. She woke and turned a piercing gaze on him.

The sleeper gave her name as Brynhild the Valkyrie, praised the light of day and the beauty of the world, and lamented the long sleep into which Odin had cast her. She had gone to a mortal battle where Odin had already decreed which side should have the victory, but had looked with favor on the leader doomed to die and she slew the man whom Odin had chosen as victor. Odin then told her that she would never again have the victory, but would sleep long and then be bound in a marriage which would bring her no joy. Brynhild, however, swore that she would never marry a man who had feared and she looked on Sigurd and thought him likely to be fearless.

Sigurd said that he had heard of her wisdom, and Brynhild offered to teach him the runes that gave skill in battle, safety on the sea, victory in arguments, clear-headedness in liquor and skill in healing. Sigurd was eager to learn all she would teach, although she warned that there was danger in the learning. He learned from her and loved her, and they pledged to love each other always and to marry. Sigurd rode away to the castle of King Heimir, Brynhild's foster-father in the mortal world. He was welcomed and honored there. Brynhild followed him and they loved each other well, but she was in no haste to lay aside her horse, armor and weapons and become a wife, and more than once she warned him that he would marry another and cause great misery. Sigurd swore that he would do no such thing, and he gave her Andvare's cursed ring as a token of love.

    The report of Sigurd's courage, strength, courtesy and good looks spread far and wide, and Heimir's neighbors King Giuki and Queen Grimhild invited Sigurd to visit their court. He was made welcome there and loved by all- most of all by Gudrun, Giuki and Grimhild's daughter. Queen Grimhild heard Sigurd speak often of his love for Brynhild, but she resolved that he would nevertheless marry Gudrun. She was skilled in magic, and she brewed him a drink which caused him to forget Brynhild completely. Then she offered him Gudrun's hand in marriage, and Sigurd accepted with joy. Gudrun's eldest brothers swore oaths of brotherhood to Sigurd, and Grimhild taught him the magic skill of shape-changing as she had taught it to her own children. Sigurd fathered a son and a daughter with Gudrun, led Giuki's army in many raids and battles and never thought of returning to Heimir's court. Nor did he know that Brynhild in his absence had borne him a daughter.

Grimhild wanted to see her sons well married as well as her daughter, and she urged her firstborn, Gunnar, to court Brynhild. So Gunnar rode away to woo her, accompanied by his sworn brother Sigurd.

Now since Sigurd had left, Brynhild had refused all offers of marriage although her brother, the king Atli, had tried to make her marry to gain him strong allies. She would not agree to marry at his word, and he would not agree to let her stay always unmarried, At last they reached an agreement. When there was war she rode with the warriors. When there was peace she went back to her castle on the high fells and caused a ring of enchanted flames to burn high around it, and she swore that she would marry only the man who dared to ride to her through the flames. She thought in her heart that only Sigurd would dare to come to her so.

Gunnar steeled himself to face the fire, but his horse shied and baulked and could not be coaxed or forced into the flames. So Gunnar asked that he might ride Sigurd's grey stallion, Odin's choice for him. Sigurd agreed, but that horse would carry no man but Sigurd. At last they used the magic Grimhild had taught them to exchange shapes. Now Sigurd's face and body were those of Gunnar, but his mind and voice were the mind of Sigurd. His horse still knew him and they rode straight at the wall of flames, which rose and crackled all the more fiercely as they rode up to it. But Sigurd struck his stallion with his sword to force him through, and as they touched the flame it died before them so they rode through unscathed.

When Brynhild saw that her guest was Gunnar she was reluctant to marry him, but 'Gunnar' pled that she had sworn to marry the one who passed through the flame so she gave herself to him. They passed three nights together, but each night Sigurd laid his sword between them in the bed, saying that he had to do this to ward off a curse that was laid on him. Brynhild gave Andvare's ring to him, not knowing that she had given it back to its first owner. Nor did Sigurd remember where she had gotten that ring, for Grimhild's spell still darkened his memory.

When the three days were over Sigurd rode back to Gunnar, and each man took on his own shape again. Then Heimir gave Brynhild and Gunnar a great wedding feast where Gudrun and Brynhild drank and laughed together. But as he saw them side by side, the spell on Sigurd broke and he remembered how he had loved Brynhild.

V. The End of the Curse

One day Brynhild and Gudrun fell to quarreling about the merits of their husbands. Brynhild said Gunnar was the bravest man living, for he had passed through the fire. Gudrun laughed scornfully and said that Gunnar never did any such thing, that this brave deed like many others rightly belonged to Sigurd. She said that for the wooing he had taken Gunnar's shape, and she showed Brynhild Andvare's ring which Sigurd had given to her after the wedding feast.

Brynhild turned as white as a corpse, and she was silent all that day and the following night. The next day Gudrun taunted her, and they quarreled hotly. Brynhild accused Gudrun of deceiving Sigurd with spells, and Gudrun accused Brynhild of giving herself to Sigurd like a wanton before she was married.

Brynhild was sick with grief, and she cursed Gunnar her husband and swore never to give him joy or comfort again. She shut herself into her chamber, and all feared that she would kill herself. When Sigurd spoke at her door she let him in and cursed him for his faithlessness. He pled that he had been placed under a spell and had known nothing. He begged her to live and forgive him, and he offered to put Gudrun aside and marry Brynhild. Brynhild answered that it would do no good for him to break his vows to Gudrun as he had broken his vows to her, that she herself had sworn her oath to Gunnar and would not break it and that there was no way out but her own death and Sigurd's. Later she said the same thing to her husband, vowing to leave him if he did not kill Sigurd. Gunnar was desperate then for he had pledged to be a brother to Sigurd, but he thought he would be shamed in all men's sight if his wife left him. He also reflected that, if Sigurd died, the dragon-treasure would be his. So he promised honor and treasure to his young brother Guttorm, who had sworn no oaths to Sigurd, and Guttorm crept into Sigurd's bedchamber and gave him a death-blow in his sleep. Sigurd awoke in time to kill his killer but far too late to save himself.

Brynhild who had hated him wept for him then, and she killed herself in grief for him. But Andvare's ring and all the cursed treasure passed into the hands of Gunnar and his brothers, and the curse went with it.

Gudrun, at the insistence of her kin, married Brynhild's brother Atli who coveted the gold that had been Sigurd's. He invited Gunnar and his brothers to come to his court as honored guests and to receive both lands and treasures, and because of Gunnar's pride he agreed. But Gunnar's wife and the wives of his brothers had evil dreams and warned the king that Atli meant to betray them. Gunnar would not take back his acceptance of Atli's invitation for fear of being called a coward, but before they rode to Atli's court they hid Andvare's gold in the depths of a river in a lonely place.

Atli ambushed them as the women had foreseen, and in the fighting that followed Gunnar, his brothers and all Atli's house died, and the secret of the hoard was lost. Somewhere in the wilderness it may be that the gold still lays hidden, waiting for another finder—and that the curse waits as well.

Chapter 9: The Death of Balder

Andvare's curse did great harm in the world of men, but perhaps even the brief possession of it cursed the gods as well. After that time Odin and Loki's lives were darkened, as this tale tells.

Balder, Odin and Frigga's son, was the most beautiful and beloved of all the gods and for long ages his dwelling was a place of peace and joy. But a time came when Balder was troubled by evil dreams and filled with fear and sorrow. Then Odin, fearing for his dearest son, rode out of Asgard to Helheim, the world of the dead, where he saw a great feast being prepared. He did not go into Helheim's great hall, but by its gates he summoned an enchantress to rise from her grave and tell him the meaning of Balder's dreams. (Odin could see all that passed in the Nine Worlds as it happened, but foretelling the future seems always to have been a woman's gift.) Concealing his own name and nature and putting off his real question for a moment, he asked her what Helheim's folk were preparing to celebrate. "The arrival of Balder," she said.

In his grief and anxiety Odin sought to question her more closely, but she perceived who he was and refused to speak to any of the gods again until Loki should come to raise the giants against the gods at Ragnarok.

Odin hurried home and told the gods that he had heard that Balder must die. Frigga, his mother, was gravely distressed and she traveled throughout the worlds, taking oaths from all things that might be made into weapons or cause destruction- from metal and stone, from fire and water, from every strong tree, from every beast and bird and from every poison and sickness-oaths that they would never harm Balder. At last she rode back to Asgard, content, and announced what she had done.

Then the gods made a game of what they had feared, and often they gathered to cast weapons of all kinds at Balder and laugh to see him unhurt by all. But Loki disguised himself as a woman and came before Frigga to ask her what game the gods were playing. She told him. He appeared impressed and asked "Have all things really sworn not to harm Balder?" Frigga said that all things that mattered had sworn; there was a little shrub called mistletoe that seemed too young and small to pose a danger or to swear an oath. Then the woman left Frigga and took on Loki's shape again. Loki found where the mistletoe grew, and he carved an arrow from it. Then he hurried back to where the gods still cast their weapons at Balder.

One god, Hoder, sat sadly apart from the others. Loki went up to him and asked why he did not join in the game. Hoder answered that his blindness made it impossible. Loki then gave him the mistletoe dart and promised to guide his hand, saying that surely all the gods should take part in honoring Balder by showing his invincibility. Hoder agreed happily and took the shot. The arrow, guided by Loki, struck Balder in the heart and Balder fell dead to the ground.

The gods were overwhelmed with sorrow and horror. Frigga cried out for someone to win her love by riding into Helheim and trying to bring Balder back, and Odin's young son Hermod agreed to make the journey. They set Balder's body in a ship, together with that of his wife Nanna who had died of grief at his loss, and they set fire to that ship and sent it out over the sea.

Hermod rode nine days and nights through dark cold places, crossed the narrow bridge and leaped the great gate and finally came to the hall of Helheim. Going in, he saw his brother Balder seated in the place of honor with a face full of sorrow. Hel the goddess, the mistress of the world of Helheim, sat at Balder's side. Hermod knelt before her, told her how everything in all the worlds grieved for Balder, and begged her to let Balder return with him to Asgard. Hel answered that she would let Balder go only if Hermod could prove the truth of his words by having everything in the world weep for Balder.

Hermod rode back to the gods with Hel's demand, and soon messengers were sent to every being in the worlds. Gods, men and elves, beasts and birds and trees and stones all wept for Balder's loss. But one messenger stopped at a cave where a great giantess sat alone, and when she heard his words she refused to mourn for Balder. "Neither in life nor death did he give me gladness," she said. "Let Hel keep what she has!" She could not be persuaded, so the messenger rode home in sorrow and reported that their last hope was gone, and Balder would remain among the dead.

Now all the gods desperately grieved and Odin was also afraid, for in Balder's death he saw the beginning of the ruin of Asgard and of the entire world. As the gods talked over the causes of their grief they realized that it was Loki who had learned of the one thing which had not vowed to harm Balder, Loki who had made the mistletoe dart and Loki disguised as a giantess, who had refused to weep for Balder. Loki fled, but the gods caught him and bound him to the rocks beneath a serpent that dropped venom onto his face. Loki's wife Sigyn stayed with him and caught the falling poison in a cup to spare him pain, and while the cup was filling Loki plotted vengeance. But whenever the cup filled Sigyn had to turn aside to empty it and the venom fell on Loki's face, he writhed so in his pain that the world was shaken with earthquakes. It may be that Loki wept then but never for Balder, only for himself.

Chapter 10: The End and the Beginning

These stories and many more were told as tales of the past. But there was one story always left in the future, glimpsed only through prophecy. That was the tale of Ragnarok, the doom of the gods and the end of the world.

Odin kept Ragnarok always in mind. He traveled far and wide seeking the visions of seers so that he might know what would happen; he gave up his right eye for the Water of Wisdom so that he might learn how best to defend the worlds from destruction; he kept and trained his dead heroes in Valhalla to take part in that great battle. But he knew, always, that all his wisdom and strength could not save him or Asgard in the end.

Like all prophecies of the end, the predictions of Ragnarok were many, varied, and sometimes obscure. But this much was known:

At the end chaos would burst forth to overwhelm the order that the gods had made and preserved. In Midgard the end would begin with three winters of war and general lawlessness; men would fight without mercy, murder one another and betray their own kin through adultery and with violence. After this would come three years of winter, with the sun's warmth weakened and terrible winds sweeping the earth so that its people died of hunger. Then the wolves that ran behind the moon and sun would overtake them, and darkness would fall on the land.

In Asgard Loki would break from his bonds and so would his son, the wolf Fenrir. In the depths of the sea Loki's other monster-son, the Midgard Serpent, would rise in anger. The giants out of Jotunheim and the fire-demons out of Muspelheim would come to Loki's call and attack the gods. The battle would be desperate. Thor would kill and be killed by the Midgard Serpent, and Heimdall the sentry of Asgard would kill and be killed by Loki. Odin would fight against the wolf Fenrir and die, but his son Vidar would destroy the wolf. At the end, when the best part of both armies lay dead, Surt the fire-bearer would come from the burning world of Muspelheim and set Asgard, Midgard and the World Tree itself ablaze. The sea would rise, churned up by the death-throes of the Midgard Serpent, and the ruined land would be drowned.

But this destruction, while great and terrible, was not quite final. Out of the empty seas land would rise again and green plants would grow there; indeed, fine crops of grain would grow without any man tending them. Balder would return from the dead, Honir would return with the gift of prophecy added to his other strengths, and Thor's sons would arise carrying their father's great hammer. Soli would not return from death to drive the chariot of the sun but her daughter, even stronger and lovelier than she, would rise and give light to the worlds again. And a man and a woman, long concealed in a safe place hidden from the ruin, would emerge to drink of the dew and eat of the plants of the field and start the human race again. Some said also that the dead humans in Helheim would be raised to life again, but some said otherwise.

What would be the end of this new world? That also was unclear. Some said that this healed and blessed earth would endure forever in beauty. But the seer who told Odin most about the end and the new beginning went on from describing Balder's rebirth and the green land to speak of a devouring dragon rising from the earth with its mouth full of dead men. Then she refused to speak more. All that seemed certain was that there would be a new beginning.

Afterword: Sources

This is only a sampling of the rich and diverse collection of Norse myths. Retellings of the myths abound, some more faithful to the original sources than others. The primary sources of Norse mythology are the Eddas and the Volsungasaga.

The Poetic Eddas, or Elder Eddas, are a collection of tales and poems by anonymous poets, gathered from various sources and often contradicting each other. There are dramatic stories, collections of advice, bewildering prophecies, lore-rhymes full of names and etymologies, trash-talk contests between various gods and more. Henry Adams Bellows' English translation, with copious notes, is available online.

The Prose Edda, or Younger Edda, brings together oral-tradition legends and written ballads to make some kind of coherent account of Norse cosmology and legend. It also makes some additions and alterations in an attempt to harmonize the Norse mythology with Christianity. Rasmus Anderson's translation of the Prose Edda is available online free of charge from Project Gutenberg.

The Volsungasaga tells the story of the Cursed Hoard in considerable depth, incorporating the fragments of the story which occur in the Elder Edda. William Morris and Eirikr Magnusson's translation is available online from Project Gutenberg.

Printed in Great Britain
by Amazon